DEMCO

SOUTHERN ELEPHANT SEAL

GIANTS AMONG US

Jason Cooper

Rourke Book Co., Inc.
Vero Beach, Florida 32964

Edited by Pamela J.P. Schroeder

PHOTO CREDITS
All photos © Lynn M. Stone

Library of Congress Cataloging-in-Publication Data
Cooper, Jason, 1942-
   Southern elephant seal / by Jason Cooper.
      p. cm. — (Giants among us)
   Includes index.
   Summary: Describes the physical characteristics, habitat, and
behavior of this huge marine mammal.
   ISBN 1-55916-188-4
   1. Southern elephant seal—Juvenile literature. [1. Southern
elephant seal. 2. Seals (Animals)] I. Title. II. Series: Cooper,
Jason, 1942- Giants among us.
QL737.P64C65   1997
599.79'4—dc21   96-52193
                                       CIP
                                       AC

Printed in the USA

TABLE OF CONTENTS

SOUTHERN ELEPHANT SEAL

Elephant seals are among the real giants of earth and sea. No, they aren't as big as great whales, but they are huge **marine** (muh REEN), or saltwater, mammals. Southern elephant seals are the largest of the world's 33 **species** (SPEE sheez), or kinds, of seals.

Elephant seals earned their name with size and snout. The male elephant seal's long snout looks like the beginning of a trunk. The seal can blow up the snout with air, like a balloon.

A male elephant seal's snout can fill with air and stand out like a short trunk.

ELEPHANTS OF THE SEA

Most male mammals are larger than their mates. It is not surprising that a male, or bull, elephant seal is bigger, too. It's how much bigger he is that's amazing!

A female, or cow, southern elephant seal is a heavyweight herself. She may be 9 feet (2.7 meters) long and weigh 2,000 pounds (901 kilograms).

A big male southern elephant seal makes his mate look like a midget. He may be 15 feet (4.6 m) long and weigh more than 8,000 pounds (3,603 kg)—more than a rhino.

A southern elephant seal bull may outweigh its mate by 6,000 pounds (2,702 kg)!

WHERE SOUTHERN ELEPHANT SEALS LIVE

Elephant seals spend most of their lives in the ocean. They crawl ashore to have pups and **molt** (MOLT). When seals molt, old patches of skin and hair peel away. New skin and hair replaces the old.

Southern elephant seals live in and around the icy oceans at the southern tip of the world. Most of these seals raise their pups on islands within 1,000 miles (1,612 kilometers) of Antarctica.

Southern elephant seal pups share a beach with king penguins on cold, snowy South Georgia Island.

PUPS, THE BABY SEALS

Southern elephant seal pups are born in October. October is springtime in the Antarctic.

Pups are little giants even at birth. A newborn southern elephant seal may weigh 100 pounds (45 kg)!

Pups look like fat, furry bullets with flippers. They grow quickly for three weeks feeding on fat-rich mother's milk. Then they live off **blubber** (BLUH ber), or fat, for a month before going into the ocean.

Southern elephant seal pups, now on their own, rest on a grassy beach.

Southern elephant seals splash into the surf of the Antarctic Ocean.

Fights between elephant seal bulls are often bloody. The seals' thick blubber usually prevents serious injuries.

PREDATOR AND PREY

Elephant seal pups have no real enemies on land. However, they do face danger all the time. The huge adults sometimes crawl over them and crush them to death.

At sea, young elephant seals can be **prey** (PRAY), or food, for larger **predators** (PRED a torz). Great white sharks, leopard seals, and orcas (killer whales) attack elephant seals.

Elephant seals hunt octopus and squid. They also eat fish, crabs, and small, crusty marine creatures.

This sleepy southern elephant seal pup will soon leave land for the sea. It has survived the dangers of life in a seal colony.

ELEPHANT SEAL HABITS

Elephant seals gather in large groups when they come ashore. The groups are called **colonies** (KAHL uh neez). Colonies are noisy places. Elephant seals grunt, burp, and bellow loudly.

Elephant seals at sea travel hundreds of miles to find food. Except for nursing pups, elephant seals eat only in the sea.

Elephant seals find prey by diving. They are the deepest divers of all seals. An elephant seal can dive a mile (1.6 km) deep!

Elephant seal colonies, like this one on Antarctica, are noisy, crowded places.

ELEPHANT SEAL COUSINS

The southern elephant seals' closest cousin is a look-alike, the northern elephant seal. It too is a giant, weighing up to 6,000 pounds (2,700 kg). This butterball is the second largest seal. A walrus weighs up to 3,800 pounds (1,712 kg).

Northern elephant seals live along the Pacific Coast of North America from Vancouver Island, Canada, to Cedros Island, Mexico. A growing colony lives on the California coast at Año Nuevo.

A molting northern elephant seal bull on the beach at Año Nuevo, California, bellows. The seal's old, peeling skin is being replaced by a new layer.

PEOPLE AND ELEPHANT SEALS

People used to kill southern elephant seals in huge numbers. Elephant seal fur was not valuable, but their oily blubber was. Seal hunters made thousands of gallons of oil by boiling elephant seals' blubber. In the 1800s, seal oil was valuable fuel for heat and light. Later, the oil was used in the food industry.

By the end of the 1800s, hunters had nearly wiped out southern elephant seals. When the colonies started to grow, hunting began again. Hunting finally ended for good in 1964.

Southern elephant seals and penguins share Antarctic beaches with people who have come to watch, not hunt.

SAVING ELEPHANT SEALS

The birds and mammals of the islands and seas around Antarctica are protected from hunting. The healthy southern elephant seal population has grown to about 750,000. The largest colonies are on cold, snowy South Georgia Island, about 800 miles (1,296 km) from Antarctica.

Northern elephant seals are also protected. Their number is well above 100,000 and growing.

Elephant seals will survive as long as their colonies and food supplies in the oceans are protected.

Glossary

blubber (BLUH ber) — a layer of fat that helps keep animals warm in very cold climates

colony (KAHL uh nee) — a group of animals of the same kind living together

marine (muh REEN) — of or relating to the ocean, salt water

molt (MOLT) — the process of growing new skin, feathers, or fur in place of old

predator (PRED a tor) — an animal that hunts other animals for food

prey (PRAY) — an animal that is hunted by another animal for food

species (SPEE sheez) — within a group of closely-related animals, one certain kind, such as a *southern* elephant seal

INDEX